From Trafficked to Trucking

A Survivor's Journey to Drive Change

DollFace

Get It Done Publishing, LLC. Atlanta, GA 30349
www.getitdonepublishing.com

Printed in the United States of America.
Paperback ISBN: 978-1-952561-28-3

Contents

Introduction

After enduring years of unspeakable abuse at the hands of my captors, trapped in the world of human trafficking and domestic violence, I found a glimmer of hope and a path to freedom in the unlikely form of the trucking industry, where the open road became my sanctuary and my escape from the horrors of my past. At first, I was hesitant. Trucking seemed like a challenging, male-dominated industry, and I wasn't sure if I wanted to be around more men or if I even had what it took to be a trucker, but I had no other options. I had to do what I needed to do by any means necessary; it was a matter of life or death.

Today, I'm proud to say I'm a successful truck driver. The road hasn't always been easy, but it has been a journey of self-discovery, healing, and redemption. Through trucking, I've found a sense of purpose, independence, and freedom I never thought possible.

This book will give you a glimpse of my survival from being trafficked to being a successful truck driver and mentor in the trucking industry. I will outline trafficking and domestic violence statistics and how the trucking industry can play a vital role in breaking the cycle of abuse. Most importantly, I will show you how your support can help survivors break free from the bondage of sex trafficking and domestic violence and put them on the road to a fresh start by utilizing the trucking industry.

So, come along for the ride. Get a glimpse into my life as a survivor and trucking influencer. Let me show you how trucking can not only save lives but transform lives, just as it did mine.

Blindspot: On the Road to Recovery

I was raised in Las Vegas, Nevada, under the limelight of sex and drugs. From a young age, I had been a victim of child molestation and abuse. Growing up in an unstable environment, with my mother being addicted to drugs and my brother a pimp, being molested and abused became a normal thing for me. Surrounded by drug addicts with no sense of security, structure, discipline, or role model in my home, I found myself pregnant at sixteen.

Being a teen mom having the maternal instinct to create a safe environment for my daughter, I sought stability. Something I had never experienced but owed to my child. It seemed like an impossible feat because my mother's words lived rent-free in my mind that "no man wants a readymade family," so I figured no man would want me. However, to my surprise, I ended up in a relationship.

It wasn't a whirlwind romance, but things were going well until my boyfriend came into the room one night and laid in my bed while I slept. He would only touch me while I was asleep, never while I was awake. If I started to wake up, he would stop. He started fondling me, and I could feel him getting aroused. I was paralyzed by fear. I couldn't move, and I didn't desire to be touched, but growing up, my mom would yell at me in her drunken state after being with a John, "If you ain't giving your man sex, he'll get it from somewhere." So, I lay still, scared, pretending to be asleep as he molested me. That night I conceived my second child.

I held back tears and continued in the relationship. At least I had someone. Someone that wanted me and only me—at least I thought. When I discovered he molested my daughter, the line was drawn, and I had had enough. The cops were called, he confessed, and was placed in jail.

Hurt and homeless with two kids, I had no time to sulk in my emotions. I was responsible for the well-being and safety of my children, and I still desired stability. I was able to find a shelter that would take my family in and landed a job working at a call center. It was at my place of employment that I met someone. I conceived my third child, and we had a great relationship. However, our relationship was off and on, and during one of our off periods, he walked out. I truly believed we were over. He was the only good thing in my life, and he left.

Feeling hopeless and desperate for money to take care of my family, I turned to the streets for quick money. I met a guy who sold me dreams of taking care of my children and I. It was a dream that was too good to be true because he kidnapped me, held me against my will, and pimped me out to the highest bidder. He was considered a "Romeo Pimp," he groomed me, lured me into a romantic relationship, and made me fall in love with him. He had me wrapped around his finger. That was his way of taking care of me. The first night he listed me on a sex-for-sale Internet site, I was raped by a John. It wasn't until I got arrested for prostitution that I found out I was pregnant with my fourth child. I traded one hell hole for another.

Desperate for a way out, an unfortunate fate struck. I was involved in a car accident that allowed me to escape my abuser. Hurt but relieved, I was able to get a fresh start. I pursued a college degree in criminal justice, found employment, and seemed to be on a path to recovery and healing when I got involved in another relationship. He seemed protective and affectionate. I thought we had equal input and say regarding our relationship. He made good money, and seemed like an upstanding gentleman, but over time, I saw the wolf in sheep's clothing. The scales were unbalanced. The protection and affection were a disguise for his controlling, manipulative, and narcissistic behavior, and again, I found myself coerced back into the world of being sex trafficked. He was considered a combination of both a Romeo Pimp and a "Gorilla Pimp." Using physical violence and coercion to control me.

Fearing for my life, I sought refuge in a casino where I was previously arrested for trespassing—causing me to have a criminal record and creating a barrier for me to secure stable employment.

Free from my abuser but not the cycle of abuse, I constructed a plan to escape the lifestyle altogether. Through Workforce Solutions, I was able to secure my CDL permit, eventually got my commercial driver's license, and became a truck driver.

After graduating from the University of Nevada Las Vegas, I left Las Vegas to escape trafficking and abuse. As a truck driver, I had the capability to relocate to Texas, where I began making connections within the trucking industry through social media.

Using the handle "DollFace," I adopted the name given to me by my trafficker to show that he no longer had control over me. My social media presence soon attracted the attention of the trucking community. It led to opportunities for me to speak and mentor other women, particularly survivors of human trafficking and domestic violence.

I became a mentor and brand ambassador for the S.H.E. Trucking organization, which provided me with love, support, and connections for my advocacy work. In addition to the above, I am a driver trainer, trucking mentor, and consultant.

Logbook: The Problem and Statistics

The Problem

Survivors of human trafficking and domestic violence often face a range of complex physical, emotional, and psychological barriers that can make it difficult for them to leave their abusers or traffickers. These barriers include fear of retaliation, financial dependence, lack of support networks, and emotional manipulation.

Regarding securing employment, survivors may have gaps in their work history or lack the necessary skills and education to obtain stable jobs.

Additionally, their abusers or traffickers may have controlled their access to money and resources, making it tough to secure housing or transportation. Survivors may also struggle with mental health issues, such as PTSD and anxiety, making it challenging to maintain employment or pursue education and training.

In terms of safety, survivors may fear for their physical safety and the safety of their loved ones if they leave their abusers or traffickers. They may also face threats of retaliation, stalking, or harassment.

Finally, when it comes to financial stability, survivors may face significant financial barriers, such as debt, lack of access to credit or banking, and limited job opportunities. These barriers can make it difficult for survivors to achieve financial independence and stability, which are essential for breaking free from the cycle of abuse and exploitation.

Statistics

According to the International Labour Organization, there are an estimated 40.3 million victims of human trafficking globally[1]. Of these, 81% are trapped in forced labor, while 25% are children.

In the United States, an estimated 17,500 people are trafficked into the country every year, and around 300,000 American children are at risk[2] of being trafficked each year, according to the Department of Homeland Security.

The National Domestic Violence Hotline reports that, on average, nearly 20 people per minute are physically abused by an intimate partner in the United States. This equates to more than 10 million women and men annually[3]. The same organization reports that financial abuse occurs in 98% of abusive relationships, with the abuser controlling the victim's access to money, employment, and other resources.

These statistics highlight the prevalence and severity of these issues and the challenges that survivors face in securing employment, safety, and financial stability.

1. Human trafficking argument topics. 100+ Argumentative Essay Topics .... http://alertservice-d.grundfos.com/human-trafficking-argument-topics.html
2. Student work sheds light on hotels' dark side: sex trafficking. https://news.cornell.edu/stories/2017/06/student-work-sheds-light-hotels-dark-side-sex-trafficking
3. FEW Women's Health: Domestic Violence Awareness. (2020). In FEW's News (Vol. 52, Issue 3, p. 6). Federally Employed Women, Inc.

Anchor It: Driving Change

<u>How I Am Driving Change</u>

I am dedicated to breaking the cycle of violence and abuse by advocating for and mentoring other survivors of human trafficking and domestic violence, empowering them to reclaim their lives and gain financial freedom through the trucking industry. My organization will foster a safe and supportive environment and provide survivors with access to resources and support that will help them succeed and become independent while healing, growing, and thriving in their new chapter. I believe everyone deserves a chance to start a new life, and I am proud to be a part of their journey as a survivor myself.

My dedication can help with the problem of survivors of human trafficking and domestic violence leaving their partners and securing employment, safety, and financial stability in three ways:

First, my dedication to breaking the cycle of abuse by advocating for and mentoring other survivors can provide a role model and source of inspiration for those struggling to leave their abusive situations. This can encourage them to seek help and support in breaking free from their abuser.

Second, focusing on empowering survivors to gain financial freedom through the trucking industry can provide a viable career path for those who may have difficulty securing employment due to their past experiences. This can give them a sense of independence and stability that can help them rebuild their lives.

And third, my commitment to creating a comforting and encouraging environment for survivors can help address many survivors' safety concerns when leaving their abuser. By providing access to resources and support, survivors can feel more confident and secure in their decision to leave and start a new life.

How the Trucking Industry Can Drive Change

Employment in the trucking industry can help survivors of human trafficking and domestic violence in several ways:

Financial stability: Employment in the trucking industry can provide survivors of human trafficking and domestic violence with a path toward financial stability and independence, which are key factors in breaking the cycle of abuse. The trucking industry offers a range of job opportunities, from truck drivers to logistics coordinators and dispatchers, and these jobs often provide competitive salaries and benefits.

Flexibility: One of the biggest advantages of the trucking industry is its flexible schedules. Unlike the typical nine-to-five office job, life as a truck driver will not confine you to a set schedule. If you wish to begin work early in the morning and be home by late afternoon, there are plenty of jobs that will suit your preferred schedule. If you prefer to work late nights and sleep in the daytime, there are also plenty of routes that require drivers to fill those late night/early morning hours. This flexibility can provide survivors with the freedom to attend therapy sessions, take care of their children, or simply take a break when they need it most.

Independence: Moreover, the nature of the trucking industry means that survivors can have the opportunity to travel and work independently, which can provide survivors with a sense of freedom and empowerment for those who have experienced control and abuse in previous relationships. Additionally, the trucking industry has a shortage of drivers, which can provide opportunities for employment for survivors.

Support: Furthermore, the trucking industry often has a supportive community which can be important for survivors who may feel isolated and alone. Trucking companies often have programs in place to support their employees, including resources for mental health, financial management, and career advancement, which can be beneficial for survivors who may be facing additional challenges.

My objective of establishing a nurturing and encouraging atmosphere for survivors in the trucking sector can aid in tackling the obstacles they may encounter while finding employment, such as insufficient resources or connections. With the right training and support, survivors can thrive in the trucking industry and build a new life for themselves and their loved ones.

Relay: Let's Work Together to Drive Change

Help Drive Change

J oin me in driving change and breaking the cycle of abuse by supporting the mission to empower survivors of human trafficking and domestic violence through the trucking industry.

As a sponsor, your funding will help provide resources and support to survivors, creating a pathway to employment and financial stability. Your financial resources can help establish and run a nonprofit organization, enabling the organization to provide comprehensive services and support to survivors, such as job training, counseling, and access to safe housing.

As a partner, your collaboration will help expand our reach and impact and allow us to offer more comprehensive services to survivors. Your financial support will help us develop new programs and initiatives that aim to break the cycle of abuse and empower survivors to live safe, independent, and fulfilling lives.

And as a mentor, your guidance and support will

help survivors navigate the challenges of entering the trucking industry and building a new life. You can help raise awareness about the issue of human trafficking and domestic violence and the vital role that employment in the trucking industry can play in supporting survivors. Help survivors develop their skills, gain confidence, and establish a professional network in the trucking industry.

Whether through sponsorship, book purchases, or spreading the word about my story, every action helps to break the cycle of abuse and support individuals on their journey to financial freedom and independence. Join the cause and become a part of the movement to empower survivors and create a better future for all.

Together, we can make a difference in the lives of survivors and help them thrive. Use the QR code below to contact me and learn more about how you can be a part of this important work.

Bill of Lading: Benefits

There are several benefits for sponsors, partners, and mentors in supporting the mission:

Social Impact:

You will be making a meaningful impact in the lives of survivors of human trafficking and domestic violence. Your contribution will help these individuals gain financial independence and break the cycle of abuse.

Brand Visibility:

With your logo displayed on our marketing material, you will demonstrate your commitment to making a positive change in society. You will be able to show your customers and employees that you care about social issues and are taking action to address them.

Networking Opportunities:

You will be able to network with other like-minded organizations and individuals who share your commitment to social impact. You may also have the opportunity to connect with survivors of human trafficking and domestic violence and learn more about their experiences.

Mentorship Opportunities:

Make a significant impact on the life of a survivor by sharing your knowledge and experience. You can help guide them toward success in the trucking industry and beyond.

Personal Fulfillment:

Make a positive difference in the world and help individuals who have experienced significant trauma. This can provide a sense of personal fulfillment and satisfaction that is difficult to achieve through other means.

By supporting the mission to help survivors of human trafficking and domestic violence enter the trucking industry, you will be making a meaningful impact on society, increasing brand visibility, networking with like-minded individuals, creating mentorship opportunities, and experiencing personal fulfillment.

Landing Gear: Conclusion

I wanted to do something completely untraditional and different. From the bottom of my heart, I want to thank you. The fact that you are holding this book lets me know that you want to support the cause. Together we can drive change and support the effort to fight human trafficking and domestic violence and help survivors reclaim their lives by bringing them into the trucking industry and away from the cycle of human trafficking and domestic violence. Your support deserves a standing ovation and a round of applause. Thank you for taking the time to learn more about me and this global issue we all have a moral duty to solve.

Are you aware of Maslow's Hierarchy of Needs? Without going into too much detail, his theory states we have a hierarchy of needs from basic to complex that needs to be met for us to be happy and what one would do to achieve that happiness. The hierarchy starts with the most basic of needs vital for survival, physiological needs, and ends with self-actualization.

The first two basic needs are physiological and safety

needs. Physiological needs are things such as air, water, food, shelter, clothing, and sleep; safety includes personal security, employment, resources, health, and property. One cannot go to the next hierarchy without fulfilling the one prior to it.

Would you be willing to help someone by providing them with the basic needs (food, water, shelter, or safety) they lack and are unable to provide for themselves, especially those who have experienced abuse and neglect, or would you turn away and ignore it because it's not your problem?

From a very young age, I experienced abuse, molestation, and rape. I was abused by everyone in my life except my father, who was unaware of what was going on. My mother had a lot of men in her life, most of whom raped and molested me. She even sold me for sex, and when I told my pimp brother what happened (hoping for his protection), but he didn't believe me. Instead, he blamed me for it, saying I probably seduced him. Hearing him say that hurt me to my core; my brother was my knight and shining armor. I wanted, and so desperately needed, him to be my protector, but he only let me down.

Being around my brother, I saw first-hand what gorilla pimps, a.k.a. traffickers, did to their victims and the consequences if their victims didn't do what they were told. I saw him beat women to a pulp right in front of my eyes. He used violence and coercion to control those women. Being in that environment was normal for me, but deep down inside, I knew I would end up just like them. I needed a safe haven, an escape. I yearned for love, safety, and stability. I yearned for the basic needs most people take for granted.

I turned to a pastor and first lady at a local church for help, but they didn't provide any assistance. Probably because my mother was to busy sleeping with the pastor; his wife chastised and blamed me for everything wrong in her marriage. She even blamed me for my abuse, which was not only unhelpful but also further traumatizing. I literally had no one to turn to for support. In my most despairing moments, I wondered if anyone even cared about my life. I was heading in a dangerous direction.

I eventually found help through strangers, organizations, and nonprofits. Had it not been for them, I would have been just another statistic. A poor black prostitute who died, leaving four children to be given to the system. They would become another statistic, and I wouldn't be alive today to tell my story. Thanks to their assistance, I now have the platform and the ability to help others. It is my moral duty to give back and help survivors reclaim their lives. It is a testament to my strength and resilience that I was able to find an escape plan in the trucking industry and start to turn my life around despite all the adversity and challenges I faced. I survived and strived.

My story is a heartbreaking reminder of the dangers of human trafficking and the devastating impact it can have on its victims. Like myself, survivors have a hard time escaping the cycle of abuse because they depend on their abusers for everything. We don't have work skills, do not truly know how to care for ourselves, and are afraid, embarrassed, or ashamed to ask for help. I had to remind myself that seeking help and support is not a sign of weakness but rather a sign of strength.

The next time you're driving home down that street

and you see a streetwalker walking down it, remind yourself that those victims may be underage and/or being forced to walk that street. When you're at home getting ready to eat dinner, remind yourself that a victim is being forced to get ready to sell their body for their trafficker's financial gain. When you're getting ready to go to bed and lay your head on that pillow, remind yourself that a victim is being forced to lay their head in someone's lap or their head is getting smashed in by their trafficker to keep control of them. When you wake up the next morning to get ready for work, a victim who was trafficked the night before may not be waking up either due to the hands of their trafficker or the person who paid for them.

You may say, it's not my problem; it's not in my neighborhood. But human trafficking and domestic violence can happen to anyone, regardless of age, gender, or background. Traffickers are good at hiding their victims in plain sight. Have you taken a close look at the house next door to you or on that corner down the street? Traffickers find their victims from all over, places you would least expect, such as schools, colleges, churches, and playgrounds. It's happening, but how can we recognize that it is happening, and what can we do to help? What can we do to drive change and make an impact on ending human trafficking and domestic violence? How can we help provide victims with their basic needs?

Human trafficking and domestic violence are everybody's problem. It's easy to turn away and ignore but remember that victims are suffering and need our help. It could be your mother, sister, daughter, auntie, uncle, brother, best friend, or coworker. They don't have the security or capacity to help themselves, so it's our duty to step in and take action.

The trucking industry, specifically being a truck driver, can change a survivor's life. The sleeper berth can provide safety and security to survivors. A studio apartment on wheels, always being on the move, and being paid to do so without having to worry about the trafficker finding them, not having to worry about rent and bills, not have to worry about where the next meal is going to come from, sleeping safely at night knowing they are safe and have resources to keep them safe can help them thrive and succeed. You can be instrumental in making this happen for these survivors.

Join me in driving change, scan the QR code below, or go to www.TraffickedToTrucking.com to connect with me and help me help survivors reclaim their lives by entering the trucking industry.

About the Author

DollFace is a name that represents strength, resilience, and empowerment. She is a survivor of human trafficking and domestic violence, and her life's mission is to help others reclaim their lives and achieve financial freedom through the trucking industry.

As a truck driver, social media influencer, and public speaker, she has become a leading advocate and mentor for survivors of abuse. She inspires thousands with her story of resilience and determination, encouraging people to pursue careers in trucking and take control of their financial futures.

DollFace is a powerful ally for survivors dedicated to helping them build a better life for themselves and their families. Her unique blend of skills has made her a force to be reckoned with in the trucking industry and the fight against human trafficking. This book is part one of a two-part series. To learn more about DollFace's story, pre-order your copy of part two.

www.ingramcontent.com/pod-product-compliance
Lightning Source LLC
Chambersburg PA
CBHW060605030426

42337CB00019B/3618